WINNING THE LOTTERY

Surviving Clostridium difficile

CAROL A. STEPHEN

crowecreations.ca
info@crowecreations.ca
Ottawa Canada

Winning the Lottery: Surviving Clostridium difficile
© 2019 Carol A. Stephen

First Crowe Creations edition, July 2019

Designed by Crowe Creations
Text set in Segoe UI Semilight. Headings in Tempus Sans ITC
Cover design copyright © 2019 Crowe Creations
Cover photo iStock 488999013, proxyminder

Crowe Creations
ISBN: 978-1-927058-51-0

To those who helped save my sanity along with my life.

Table of Contents

"How can you rise, if you have not burned?"
—Hiba Fatima Ahmad

Winning the Lottery

Introduction

Mark of the Phoenix

IT'S TURNED WHITE NOW, THAT SCAR. ALMOST invisible, except for the ugly pucker closest to my right wrist. If I squint at it, turn it sideways, I imagine a soaring bird, wings outstretched to meet the air, rising on a thermal. For a long time, I saw only scar and just wanted it gone. What bird could it be? Eagle? The outspread wings suggested a large bird. Wait. Of course. Phoenix. What other bird fits this scar so well?

I mean, it's not a birthmark, nor a childhood scar from a roller-skating accident or fall from a bike. No, this scar is only eleven years old. This scar is one visible souvenir of my so-called lottery win in October 2008, when I contracted *Clostridium difficile*, C. Difficile.

When the bacteria attacked my large colon, my immune system waged war against me. Odds were only five percent that I'd pull through, even with the ostomy surgery. Yet here I am. A friend of mine on the same recovery journey adopted the phoenix as her totem. I adopted the image for my scar.

I'm grateful to the nurses and doctors who pulled me through the life-threatening infection and ileostomy surgery. Perhaps there was the slip of a hand when placing an arterial line just below my wrist. Something amiss, and no one noticed the wound until I was awake, more than a week later. When I asked about the IV line that wasn't being used, the one held in place by a small bandage, the nurse checked, found an ugly open cut. He put a fresh bandage on, not wanting to interfere with healing, but the damage had already been done.

Before I left the hospital, doctors checked the wound, gave me some antibiotics, and that was it. I tried scar cream, but that just seemed like a waste of time and money. Eventually, the angry red faded to this white pucker, shaped like a phoenix.

Oh sure, I know it doesn't shine with the bright colors of that mythical bird's plumage. But just like the phoenix, it's a symbol of rebirth, a rising from the ashes. I like that. It's a positive image, much prettier than just calling it a scar.

It reminds me how lucky I am to be here to tell its story. A reminder that an ileostomy is a life-saving surgical procedure that gave me a second chance. It's my own mark of the phoenix.

A Worm Dreams Itself Feathers

Five hundred year pulse
in the body of bird,

'til its time ends, and in
its last breath consumes

the scent of twigs,
cinnamon, muskroot and

myrrh, its gold-red feathers
burn to ash.

In black embers, a worm
dreams itself feathers,

dreams journey to
sanctuary of the sun, to

the egg tomb of his father's
myrrh-sealed cinders.

Renewal in the lift and whir of
phoenix wings at the sun's next rise.

One

Winning the Lottery

IT WAS 2008, SUMMER. I'D SPENT THE previous two years learning a heavy new job, while still covering my old one. A tough economy meant fewer staff to handle the work. Days stretched into late evenings, junk food for very late dinners, a chronic lack of sleep. I noticed upsets in my digestive system, but didn't have time to pay attention. Food intolerance, I thought. In August, after almost a year without a doctor, I signed on at a walk-in clinic with a great new doctor. But a phone call from her changed everything. "You have bad kidneys. Get in here on Monday. We'll start you on tests, get you scheduled with some specialists." Wow. Shock. Fear. Immediately I thought, "My life is over. I'm going to die!"

All weekend I was a wreck. I had to get to the doctor's office. I was ushered into a patient room, and sat there, worrying a tissue. Couldn't read, couldn't calm down. Finally the doctor came in, a tall white-bearded fellow calm and quick to reassure me. "We can fix this." Such a relief to hear death wasn't imminent. But there'd be lots more trauma to come.

New Way to Sing

My body was a speakeasy,
a gin joint, a trash can.
A place to stash junk food,
sweep dust under,
cover up detritus,
let it all hang out.

It turned on me, told me flat out
it was through with this treatment.
C Diff brought a bigger pain to think about.

Gutted like a fish.
Now I can say I got no guts.
Survived a rub-up against death.
Woke to mornings without sun.

My inner self asked to leave,
then changed her mind. I let her stay.
She gave me back my song. Taught
me a new way to sing it.

Journey through the Wrong End of the Telescope

A simple blood test, one more measure,
sodium levels coursing through veins. I watch
as the phlebotomist prods and pokes for that elusive
vein, slides needle in with practiced precision. The room
darkens, telescopes away through the wrong end of
    scope.

Blood reverses. No, not blood, some chemical,
some substance seeping into vein, a throb and vibrate
beyond the normal heart-pulsed beat, new energy

infuses literary goob and shrooms, moves from
vein to brain, down left arm. Fingers tingle and flex,
grasp air, forming a writer's claw around an imaginary
pen. Twenty seconds to the overwhelm, to the need
to write anything in the key of kryptonite.

A couple of months passed: I was going on a trip to Ocean Isle, North Carolina. The night before, I didn't feel well. Chills. Intestinal symptoms. Still, I was determined to go.

From Ottawa to Virginia is about a two-day trek. It was warm; we were enjoying the drive along roads where signs extolled Luray Caverns. I'd wanted to explore a cave since I was thirteen, reading about Carlsbad Caverns in New Mexico. A quick side trip. Within ten minutes, I was feeling faint, queasy. I had to sit down. After a few minutes I felt no better. I had to get out of the cave. On the surface again, I figured I'd had a reaction to the air in the cave.

Next day we arrived at Ocean Isle and settled in. For the first day or so, I was okay. I went shopping, but spent a lot of time running to the washroom. I stopped eating. I wasn't hungry. Eating just seemed to make things worse. After two or three days I stopped drinking water, too. My partner tried to force me to eat, but I just stayed in bed, watching television, sleeping. I maybe ate a couple of grapes, choked down some toast.

After five days it was time to head home. I hadn't realized how weak and ill I was. It was difficult to walk, difficult to focus, but I managed to pay the bill and get in the car. My partner was worried. I wasn't, although I didn't feel well at all.

Two

The Pinball Machine

THIRTY-FIVE HOURS LATER WE WERE BACK IN Canada. I went straight to the hospital. After that, things blur. I remember being examined, answering questions, an ambulance trip. More questions, faces hovering, bright lights. (And strangely, tingling cymbals, red cloth with fancy gold threads stitching what? My arms? My body? I was beginning to hallucinate.)

I woke up briefly, remember white bedclothes, white walls, white bandages, then sank back into sleep. I remember watching people through a window, not sure where I was. Someone asked if I wanted my hair washed, which sounded good, but I wasn't sure why. At night, I'd wake to flashing lights and semi-darkness, waking dreams or nightmares brought on by the Dilaudid they were giving me for pain. I didn't know where I was most of the time. It was like being in an animated cartoon. When I was finally fully awake, a week had passed.

My stomach felt like someone had embroidered it with coarse grass. I wasn't strong enough to look, probably afraid to. I couldn't sit up by myself. The bed was too long to push against, the sheets too slippery. How was it possible to be so weak? Why was I here?

Midnight in the Pinball Machine

"Everything became shadow."—Arthur Rimbaud

The walls close in while overhead the light glows
bright and blinding, a sun sphere in the ceiling,
faces looking down at the body.

I'm here, floating somewhere above the field of sight,
vibrating to the percussive of cymbals. My skin winces
with needle-pricks, as they embroider with their thin
    gold thread.

Everything becomes shadow, silence splintered by
    voices,
passing glimpses of white walls, shades around me in
    white clothing.
I run my fingers lightly down my belly, *feels like grass?*
before I sink back into sleep.

When I rouse, it's dark, yet around me lights winking,
unfamiliar sounds. I'm inside a pinball machine,
bathed in kaleidoscopes, and climbing. Awake but
    dreaming.

I dream snow, dream night, someone
washing my hair. Outside my door, witches
riding small Zambonis down corridors.

October passing into November. I no longer float,
I'm swimming back to shore, where
near-death is a pinball machine
inside the shadow, out-of-body.

Six Images from My Vacation

1.

Road blurs past miles skid under tires light outside
blinding stumble and weave pitstops night hours bent
>   *over*
brain fog new road, loud horns cold shiver and dark
>   *before light*
don't know where I am now don't care

2.

A circle of light. Darkness outside the circle.
Faces overhead, bright lights. I'm a body on a table.
I'm here! Am I here?

3.

I wake in white. Walls, ceilings. A cloud surround
of masks, of whiteout. Of blur inside a blizzard, before
it all goes black.

4.

Awake. Stitches lace belly.
Feet slide, useless on endless bedsheets.
Iced apple juice comes in one tube
back out the other. Much later,
chocolate pudding.

5.

They take away my blood
run it in and out of tubes.
Seven heated blankets
still not warm.

6.

Nurses come just to smile at me.
I don't know why, but
I'm not supposed to be here.
I'm supposed to be dead.

Passing from Death

Halos of light and
angels' voices surround me,

deft fingers embroider symbols
up and down my ribs,

golden spiral threads,
spells to cast off death,

return me to the light,
wisps of dream float.

I wake but cannot speak,
no memory of the precipice.

Awareness comes,
slowly I pass back into life.

This is a gift
of time and wisdom.

I have a prayer:
for strength and guidance,

for fullness of life in my time to come.

Opioid Dreams

I wake to brain fog, blurred memory, as if a fever broke
as I slept. Above, the lights dazzle, reflection of the
    tinfoil wrapped
tight around the shade. *Why am I in this place?*

More aware now, I am not sure where I am. The ring
of lamplight darkens the shadows. Figures in white
    coats
enter and leave. Someone bellows on the other side of
    the light.

Shallow laughter. And pain.
I run my fingers down my belly, stop at the spot
where the pain begins.

I have sprouted shoelaces. Or is it a tattoo?
I remember a dream of gold thread,
embroidery on my bicep. The tinkle of cymbals.

Flashing colored lights. The pinball machine.
I was trapped inside forever
climbing after the small white ball.

Dilaudid. Ileostomy. Clostridium difficile.
Pseudo toxic megacolon. This is the vocabulary
I am about to learn.

It was several days before I knew most of the answers, months before I was well enough to return to work. Before that, I'd have to learn to walk again. But first, I had to gain strength. I was on a liquid diet with a feeding tube, a breathing tube down my throat, and tubes coming out of both sides of my neck and body. I'd had an emergency ileostomy. Whatever that was.

One of the nurses explained, and I immediately wished she hadn't. I had somehow contracted C. difficile, a superbug that attacked my large colon. The infection was so bad that my immune system had attacked my body. My brother was told I had a five percent chance to live, with or without surgery, but the doctors recommended the operation to remove all of the infection. So, there I was in ICU, wearing what looked like a Ziploc® bag on my tummy, in isolation. Afraid to move.

Over the next few days I gradually came to understand how ill I'd been. Nurses and young doctors I didn't know stopped by to tell me how wonderful I looked, what a miracle it was. Not for me! By the time I woke up, it was all over. Well, the infection and surgery were over. But the trauma was not.

I began to pray for removal of the breathing tube. I couldn't talk, and it pressed on my lips, painful enough to bring me to tears. The nurses thought I was trying to remove it, but I was only trying to relieve the pressure and ease the pain. Did I want the tube out? I nodded vigorously. But first, I had to agree to another tube through my nose to drain fluid from my stomach. At that point I was willing to agree to anything to see the last of the tubes!

As well-meaning as my nurses were, some of them didn't understand how adjusting to an ostomy pouch can be difficult at the beginning. One ICU nurse was very caring, but didn't have much experience with ostomies. Moving me around for the x-rays I needed every morning could cause the pouch to detach, spilling its contents over the sheets and over me. I cried and cried the day it happened three or four times. I felt like an adult infant, waiting for someone to come to change my "diaper."

Is this what life was going to be like from now on? At first, there were adjustments until the right combination of pouch, seal, powder, spray, tape, etc. was determined. I wondered how I was ever going to deal with this on my own.

Waiting Room, Radiology

Around you every face shows the wear of days and you
see the future in eyes that gaze through you into the
    unseen.
You know the terrors of your night thoughts, the
    obsessions—
life, aging, death. Or, worse, the slow waste of flesh and
    mind.
One old woman moans. Another screams.
Theirs is an undiscovered pain.
Across from where you wait, a third woman
covers her face with bony fingers, rolls her head from
    side to side,
pleads to no one: don't leave, oh please, don't torture
    me!
You turn aside, wonder what haunts her waking dream,
afraid somewhere deep inside, her demons wait for
    you.

Winning the Lottery the Hard Way

I'd kill myself, a friend says when I tell her.
No tight new tummy tuck, no lifted jawline.
A body part nobody talks about, too much information.

One day you aren't well, and when you wake,
a week's gone by and there's grass on your belly
and a bag of *output*, they call it. Not poop. Nor crap.
It's *output* now. The doctors tell you you've won the
    lottery.
You're still alive.

It doesn't feel like it. You don't know what happened.
You feel helpless. And one morning, an x-ray tech's
    rough handling
rips your bag away and you lie there, soaking. Hours
in your own smell and waste. An adult baby, and
there's nothing you can do.

I was always cold, except in the middle of the night, when I'd wake soaked in perspiration. I was afraid to sleep on my side, so spent most of the night on my back on a waterproof sheet. It would be months before I felt safe to sleep without one, and a long time before I realized it was adding to the night sweats. My whole system was out of whack.

It was painful being in bed all the time, yet when they finally got me up, I couldn't stand on my own. But it was wonderful to sit in a chair to eat lunch. (Or it would have been, if the food had been tastier.) I had to have a low-residue diet. My first meal, chocolate pudding, was good! The meatloaf later on was not. Still, I needed to eat to gain strength to walk to the bathroom. Until then, I couldn't go home.

After two weeks in ICU, they finally sent me to a private room on the surgical ward. Because of the C Diff. they couldn't put me in with anyone else. But I wasn't prepared for the way I'd be treated. Don't get me wrong. I wasn't a cranky patient; I wasn't demanding. I didn't need one-on-one anymore. On the surgical ward, each nurse has more to do, more patients. That was okay with me. But the worker who delivered my meals left them outside the room, and if my nurse wasn't around, my food got cold, because I couldn't get it myself.

One day, the physiotherapists left me in a chair, blocked by my table and IV pole, which I couldn't push aside. Trapped. I called for a nurse, but when came, she saw the quarantine notice, and wouldn't enter my room.

I felt subhuman. I was depressed, angry, isolated. Eventually someone helped me back to bed. I couldn't wait to go home. I didn't know how much more I could take. I felt like I'd been there forever. I'd never been treated like this.

Nighttime War Crimes at the Dilaudid Cloud Pavilion

I change into green, pop pills. When you're fifty-
    something you need every
edge. I'm not afraid of telling the truth. I love the
    excitement. Timing is everything.
One night at the Cloud Pavilion a sumo wrestler, eyes
    crinkled shut, rotates an index finger
to the crook of his opposite elbow spewing spittle and
    bacteria into stagnant air.

A dozen elderly, lifted by their sheets, flung headlong
    into sleepless torment.
Like a child torturing a slug, the relentless poking,
    prodding, irradiating.
Poisoning. Sticking with every imaginable needle until
    cured, transferred, or dead.
In the somewhere-deep brain, elderly people have not
    uttered a single sentence in years.

Even the hapless slug withdraws when prodded
    somewhere
down a snorting, sucking tube. The slightest flicker,
    lizard-like.
The heart is not the cause of pain reaching right down
    to the bone.
Slave to biochemical mutants, to ice, to glob of phlegm
    layered on a slide.

Windows thick as a thumb, move in and out with pulse-
air gusts,
near-horizontal rain. Dank and humid. Water dripping
down walls.
Children fanning miasma with bits of cardboard, skin
hot, blind to a thousand turbulent rivulets. Surviving
on catnaps and bottled rumors in a corner near an
ATM.

Machines scream the note of origami-like artistry when
plastic-wrapping the dead.
Always mopping to be done. The morgue pushing
donuts or shoveling shaved meat.
Chaos of upstairs rooms haunted by rough men who
came at all hours. Amputated limbs, hot to the
touch, all day filling garbage barrels. Walls and
windows contaminated with roasted men.

A seventy-two-year-old woman, arms and legs jerking
in rhythm, trace of white froth in her mouth. Eyes
open, glassy, born with synchronous brain activity a
few days before Christmas.
Walking through yellowing grass toward a Polish
farmhouse, breath showing white.
Shots from somewhere. To the left, the blood. Blood
streaming through trees.

In a laboratory in Germany, a Siamese cat feels for its
breastbone, aims
the syringe of potassium chloride at the enemy across
the street.

War crimes at Nuremberg surround the living snaking
    through moribund rot of years
freckled with rust. Hundreds float over streets awaiting
    a turn to perch in an inky stairwell.

Lie still here, in a farmer's cart packed onto a train to
    Berlin.
Witness elements of Salvador Dali, Franz Kafka, Edvard
    Munch and Dachau.
Five minutes to cross the River.
A breath of life arises prior to a final destination.

Poem found in the first five pages of: Goldman, Dr. Brian, *The Night Shift*, Harper, Collins Publishers Ltd., 2010, Sacco, Joseph, M.D., *Morphine, Ice Cream, Tears*, William Morrow and Company, Inc., 1989, Fink, Sheri, *Five Days at Memorial*, Crown Publishers, 2013, Graeber, Charles, *The Good Nurse*, Twelve–Hatchette Book Group, 2013, Hager, Thomas, *The Demon under the Microscope*, Harmony Books, 2006.

I felt sorry for myself. Didn't know how to change the pouch. Couldn't even empty it. That was all I needed to know to go home. Because I was quarantined, I couldn't walk around the floor; I could only walk in my room. Still, each day another tube came out. I was so happy the day the catheter was removed. Now I could go to the washroom! That meant I could learn to empty the pouch. Once I learned that, time passed quickly, and suddenly I was checking out of the place.

I was happy at first, but then began to worry. How would I get around my house? How was I going to deal with this pouch? So many questions. A social worker explained that I'd have home care every day until they could train me, and until my wound was healed. I had to prove I could walk down and up half a staircase. I was going home. I had no idea of the challenges that I'd face. How would I ever learn to live with this disability?

Three

Toilet Training

But slowly, over the next four months at home, I learned how to deal with the paraphernalia of ostomy, with leaky pouches and flanges, with diet. My body adjusted to its new plumbing. I found an online discussion group where I could ask the thousand questions that cropped up. I learned about options and made decisions about what felt right for me. I realized that I was going to live with the ostomy rather than go through another hospital stay, even a planned one. As I adjusted, the ostomy became routine. Like having a perpetual menstrual period, in a way. Perhaps a nuisance at times, but at others something I forgot I had.

I'd lost weight and the swelling I'd come home with was all gone. For spring, I bought an entire new wardrobe to show off my new svelte figure. No sign of a bulge anywhere! Over time, I found that I didn't need to carry supplies everywhere I went. I learned to change my pouch at work in the washroom if I needed to. And I needed to in the early days, but as time passed, the number of accidents diminished. I no longer had to change every three or four days.

A pouch change now, eleven years later, does me about a week. I can't remember the last time I had a leak, but now those are usually middle of the night, probably from rolling over too far and forcing a blow-out. Even those happen very rarely.

Toilet Training

You were toilet-trained before. Now you learn another
    way.
It's always there, the little bag just under your clothes.
It's there before you even learn how to paste it on.
The day you leave the hospital, all you know is how
to open it, close it, empty it. And wonder
Will I ever learn to do this?

To attach a flange that couples with the pouch. To join
    them
like a Tupperware lid, that thing which separates you
    from
the bowel they've re-routed to end on your tummy.
It might hold for a week, or only hours. It might spring
    a leak,
or blowout from the pressure of tight jeans,
or balloon from eating onions or cabbage.

Wherever you go, your first question:
Where's the washroom?
Hyperaware now of the height of toilets, the amount of
    paper,
how much soap in the dispenser. And your hands are
    always
chapped, red, cracked, or bleeding from too much
    washing.
It's been years since you slept right through the night.

There are still issues once in a while. Because I'm used to the ileostomy now, I tend to forget it. I eat things without attention. Dried fruit and grapes are my downfall, and when I indulge in both on the same day, as I have done two Christmases in a row, I soon remember. Thank goodness for my local hospital and the caring staff there. Both times they've put things right within a short time, getting me rehydrated and back in working order.

Sometimes I think about what it would be like without the ileostomy. Then I remember what the alternative would have been. Luck doesn't always come the way we might expect. For me, it came as a two-piece pouch.

http://www.cancer.org/treatment/treatmentsandside
effects/physicalsideeffects/ostomies/ileostomy
guide/ileostomy-what-is-ileostomy

Ostomy Society Canada www.ostomycanada.ca

Ottawa Ostomy Support Group
www.ottawaostomy.ca

United Ostomy Associations of America (UOAA)
www.uoaa.org

Ostomy International www.ostomyinternational.org

The Unconventional Ileostomy Guide (Found, remix poem)

An opening in the belly, the *mucosa* of your small
    intestine
like the inside of your cheek. Warm and moist, the
    stoma
has no shut-off muscle. You won't control the passage.
No nerve endings, no pain, no normal.

You need a sense of humor; you must go out of town
to find the many things to think about: length, shape,
location, scars and folds, your height and weight near
    the hipbone
nearly invisible under clothing.

Weather will change the shape of your abdomen
ruined by moisture and temperature. The skin
should always look the same as skin anywhere else,
pushing away from sticky tape.

Water will not hurt you. Water will flow into skin.
Rinse well. Hair may cause pain. Noises sound louder to
    you
than stomach rumblings. Fold your arms
across your belly over time.

Angry the first time you go out of the house:
you can't be seen under your clothes.
You need to go to the rest room less often

than you need to urinate. Think how
you'll get rid of your new partner early. Do not wait.
Sexual contact leads to talk about life.

You'll not need special clothes.
Undergarments won't harm you.
Drink beets' reddish blood. Travel
in the car trunk or back window ledge.

There are many ways to understand your life
in the language of unpeeled fruits.

Four

Learning Acceptance

FOUR MONTHS AFTER MY SURGERY, I WENT back to work, developed new routines, got back to a new version of normal. Until one June day in 2011. That day, I was unexpectedly given my walking papers from my job, or what was left of it after most of it had moved offshore. Retirement, one year early. I thought I'd love it. The way my job had shrunk had left me unsettled and with continued company-wide cuts, severance packages were looking pretty good. The reality was different.

A five-year relationship had just ended. I was on my own for the first time since my illness, worried about being alone as I grew older. Although I'd been able to ignore my health issues, suddenly they loomed larger. No longer as strong as I used to be, I couldn't always do what I'd been able to in my fifties. I wasn't ready to accept getting old.

Preliminary Diagnosis

Murmur. Backflush.
Wrong way on a one-
way. Narrowed.

Calcification. What
does moderate mean?
Sclero- or steno-sis?

Any pain? Are you
tired yet? Equipment failure,
or lack of use?

Knife and fork, or just
a different
kind of knife?
Reroute. Or excavate?
Repair or replace? Who

decides?
Are you tired now?

How many finger-pricked holes can you make,
how many bloody vials
before the weather changes?
Is that in millimeters, or millimoles and
how many moles
in a millimole?

Do the moles mind
being measured or do they
live underground
to avoid being counted?

Are they tired yet?

A Clockwork Red

There's the night of fasting, the early morning run,
a few blocks or many miles, depending.

They poke and prod arms for veins that used to
pop to attention, now gone into hiding, reluctant
to offer themselves as sacrifice to intrusive needles.
Later the bruises will rise to shimmer just beneath the
    skin.

Five vials of red pump into clear sterile tubes,
wrapped round with administrative detail: patient name,
health card number, tests required.

Inside the vials, the specimens to be spun and
    separated,
examined for the poisons swimming in the stream:
creatinine, glucose, potassium. Each deficiency, each
excess noted and recorded.

Clockwork for the last ten years, six months and
five days, the uncounted hours, minutes.

In the winter, I began to have new aches and pains. I wanted to travel but didn't think I could do it alone. I'd lost the resilience I'd had, the resilience that got me through my late husband's heart disease, through his horrendous car crash in June, 2004, and his death seven weeks later. I'd always said I was a survivor. But in 2011, I couldn't find that inner strength to draw on when things were rough going.

Asked what I fear, I don't hesitate. "Death," I say. And getting old, that's another thing to fear. One leads to the other, most times. So many of my generation are in denial. Surgery is their answer, as if a tuck here and a stitch there fools the clock. It isn't the aging face that kills you. It's the inside stuff, the tired-out organs, the mistreated stomach: too much fat and sugar to keep the pump properly primed.

But I wonder if it's really death, really aging that I fear? Maybe it's something a bit scarier. I mean, when you're dead, it won't matter. Maybe you won't even know you're going till you're gone. During sleep. But what if it doesn't happen that way?

I guess somewhere inside I am thinking about John. How his accident changed things in a moment. Dying there at the scene, and then being hammered and pounded back to life, so hard they broke most of his ribs. I still wonder how much he really knew, how much he felt beyond the pain and the delirium of infection. What about the helplessness? What if I don't die of a heart attack? What if it is instead a debilitating stroke? What if

I continue on, alive inside but unable to interact with my world? Like being buried alive, but instead of in a grave, inside your own body. Unable to walk, unable to eat, unable to speak while they keep pumping the liquids inside you to keep you alive.

That's the scary thing. That's the true fear. That and the fact that I am not done yet. I like being alive. I often sense time running out, too much left undone, so much still to do. The weight of that, instead of driving me to action, causes inertia—rather a grim state, full of fear and envy, a loss of the wider world behind my own limitations. Some limits are real, but many are creations of the fear I've had since my close brush with death in 2008.

Awareness of my own mortality has left me with a life grown smaller. Each year in winter when the aches and pains return, those thoughts loom larger. A little harder to shed.

And yet—

When John died, my friends and family were all still in Toronto, my hometown. Neighbors were good to me, but I had no close friends for support. I reached out to grief groups on the Internet. As time passed, I found myself starting to write again. It had been many years since I'd written anything. I decided to see where it would go. I made new friends. Since then, I've come to know how precious friends are, and how important it is to surround yourself with them. I learned this lesson late in life, but learn it I did. I now have many friends, both in person and on the Internet.

It's by talking with friends, sharing our worries and successes, that I'm learning to come to grips with the realities of aging. Slowly I've started to realize that my body's going through a natural process that I'm better off adapting to, rather than trying to ignore or fight. The body slows down. The body loses strength. It isn't a matter of resistance, but one of adaptation and acceptance.

It's still difficult accepting things I cannot change. I still struggle with the idea that it's not negotiable. Even so, I find I'm living as if I'm never going to die. When I look around though, with so many things I want to do, I'm overwhelmed.

It's been a slow awakening, this recognition of what I need to do to really enjoy life: acknowledge that all things end, including me. Let go of the fear holding me back from packing that box, taking that trip, writing that book. Fear and lack of mindfulness have kept me running in place instead of moving forward.

The next step, of course, is to stop beating myself up over what I haven't done, and give myself the gift of saying, "Right now, I'm doing the best that I can."

But am I really? What might the next chapter look like with a positive spin?

Five

The Next Chapter

IF THIS WERE SOMEONE ELSE'S STORY, IT might have a different color, it might be green and smell like violets. But how do you step outside the story that's been with you all your days? It sounds a little bit Alice, doesn't it?

Perhaps it's all of a piece, then. When you fear rejection, you avoid friendships, you stay away from taking risks, you build stout walls against the world. If you can't touch me, you can't hurt me either, can you? It's hard to learn the next lesson, that your body will begin to reject you. But that's what aging seems to be. Just another message that you are not who you think you are, or at least you don't remain that person all your life.

You always wanted to know the right answer. That suggests something permanent. All your life, you've seen that nothing is permanent. But you didn't learn the lesson. The body seems to be the one constant, and yet even it is constantly dying and remaking itself, cell by cell. Aging is just another face it takes.

When you were a child, you were told not to trust other girls. So you made only a very few close friends and never kept in touch when distance and time got in the way. Just like your parents before you, or at least that's how it seemed to you. Until the day you found yourself alone in a distant city, your husband dead, all your friends and family far away.

You began to reach out to others, strangers, new groups, new activities. You learned the value of friends, but some of the old habits are still there just under the surface. When you stay isolated, your world stays small. It may feel safe, but it has its own dangers. One way or another the first story is about avoiding risk of failure to be perfect: perfect answers, perfect performance, perfect friend, perfect person.

For the most part, it works. You are safe. Except from yourself and your thoughts, and how they limit your life to something small. For you, the sky is always falling. Instead, you might begin to soar, but it is a risk you have to be willing to take.

You like things comfortable, attainable, safe. You want things that involve some risk. You're smart, you learn from history. But what is history for others is not necessarily history for you. You parents died, both of them, before they reached the age you are now. Your parents and your husband had influences and experiences in life you did not have. If those things are different, why do you expect the path you take to follow theirs?

There are opportunities to head down different paths, even at this point. Take a risk. Stop being so busy holding up the sky...

Worry Bone

Behind imaginary glass, the water
rises, only my hand now breathing air.

If I could rise, stand upright, I could
breathe, but strength deserts me

under the strain of one more challenge.
Where is the resilience I called upon,

gone with the years passing, each brings
another age line, another downslope slide.

How many slips backward before there is
no returning, before the final slide into darkness?

No Promises

Today, I find no poem of promises
in these gray skies, dark at the window,
nor in this chill wind that brushes through the trees,
then dies to a memory of air.

Today, I look to the inner self for strength,
face the year uncertain, seek the healing light.
Some days it streams through a break in the clouds,
others, it finds only a sliver of doorway to pour through.

Today, the year begins. Today, I seek my inner light,
wish to hold it fast, to keep it close inside until the Earth
tilts back toward the Sun. Today, no poem of promises,
    just this:
that somewhere inside the light, new cells are forming
    in the blood.

Acknowledgements

"WINNING THE LOTTERY" AND "MARK OF THE Phoenix" appeared in slightly different form in the Winter, 2014 issue of *Ostomy Canada* magazine. ISSN 1703-1818

The poem, "Toilet Training," first appeared in the "Let Them See You Sweat" issue of *Poetry Is Dead* magazine, June, 2017, ISSN 1920-7735.

About the Author

CAROL A. STEPHEN IS AN OTTAWA AREA poet, Associate member of the League of Canadian Poets, and former member of the Tree Reading Series (Ottawa) board.

She is the author of five chapbooks: *Above the Hum of Yellow Jackets*, 2011; *Architectural Variations*, 2012; *Ink Dogs in my Shoes*, Dec. 2014; *Unhook*, 2018, catkin press, Carleton Place; *Lost Silence of the Small*, 2018, Local Gems Press, Long Island, NY. She is the co-author with JC Sulzenko of both *Breathing Mutable Air*, 2015, Nose in Book Publishing, Castlegar BC and *Slant of Light*, 2016, Nose in Book Publishing, Castlegar BC.

Carol A. Stephen's poetry appears in the May, 2017, issue of *Poetry Is Dead* and in several regional print journals and publications, anthologies, and online at Silver Birch Press, *Topology Magazine*, *The Light Ekphrastic*, and *With Painted Words*.

Contact Information:
Carol A. Stephen
cstephen0@gmail.com
Blog: http://www.quillfyre.wordpress.com